For my son, Sam—fisherman/architect.

Thanks to Jill Davis for finding a place for the book; to my agent Brenda Bowen for sealing the deal;
and to all the folks at Blue Apple Books.

Thanks to New York's Metropolitan Museum of Art, home of the sphinx of Hatshepsut.

Special thanks to Fred Sager at the Met Museum for taking me behind the scenes in the museum's mounting department.

But the BIGGEST thank-you goes to Egyptologist Isabel Stuenkel, who toured me in and about
the Met's Egyptian galleries and suggested this sphinx as a subject. She went on to answer zillions of my questions,
silly and not, and graciously pointed me to the proper galleries and antiquities from which to do my sketching.
This book could not have been done without her. –J.H.

Copyright © 2010 by Jessie Hartland
All rights reserved / CIP Data is available
Published in the United States 2010 by
🍎 Blue Apple Books
515 Valley Street, Maplewood, NJ 07040
www.blueapplebooks.com

Distributed in the U.S. by Chronicle Books
First Edition
Printed in China 09/10
ISBN: 978-1-60905-032-0

1 3 5 7 9 10 8 6 4 2

JESSIE HARTLAND

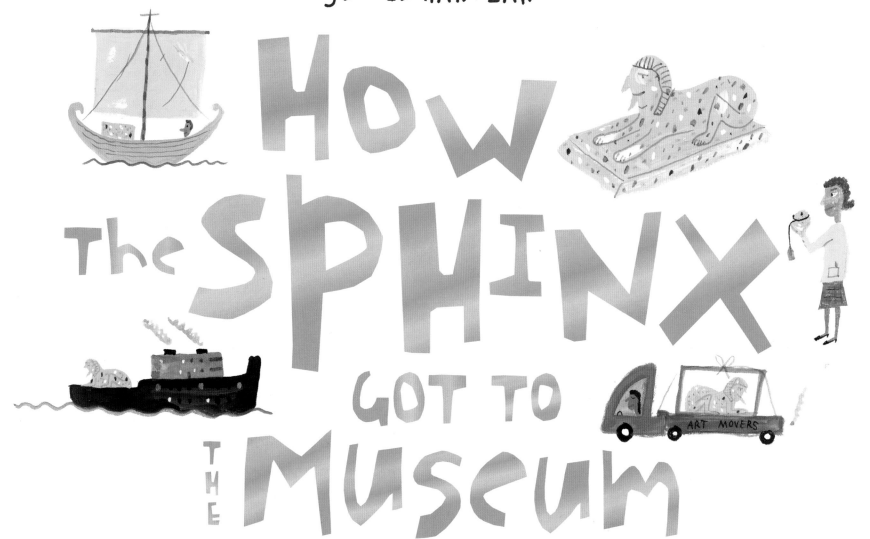

HOW THE SPHINX GOT TO THE MUSEUM

🍎 Blue Apple Books

Thousands of years ago, a pharaoh ruled Egypt. That wasn't unusual. What was unusual was that this pharaoh was a woman. Her name was Hatshepsut. Many monuments and pieces of art were created in her honor. There were statues, smooth and massive; obelisks one hundred feet tall; vessels and vases made of stone; bead-laden gold jewelry; and an enormous temple built in Thebes. Best of all, carved stone sphinxes— medium, large, and huge— stood guard in front of her temple.

In about 1470 B.C.,

PHARAOH HATSHEPSUT

meets with her architect, Senenmut,

to plan her temple . . .

and orders a collection

of statues, including

a set of six sphinxes.

The architect's assistant

takes down

the order . . .

and delivers

it to the

SCULPTOR...

who sends
his assistant
to the quarry
at Aswan . . .

to obtain
a HUGE block
of granite
to bring down
the Nile River
to Thebes.

Aswan

Thebes

Here is the **SCULPTOR**

working with mallets and chisels, carving the granite SPHINX that was . . .

ordered by the PHARAOH HATSHEPSUT.

Here are the **EGYPTIAN PRIESTS** with Hatshepsut

admiring the magnificent and massive brand new granite SPHINX that was . . .

sculpted by the SCULPTOR

and ordered by the PHARAOH.

Here is Hatshepsut's

STEPSON Thutmose III,

who becomes sole pharaoh
after she dies.

Trying to erase all trace of Hatshepsut,
he orders his workmen to hack and chop
and destroy the statues
of sandstone, limestone, and granite,
and even the SPHINX that was . . .

admired by the **EGYPTIAN PRIESTS,**

carved from granite by the **SCULPTOR**

and ordered by the **PHARAOH.**

And left undiscovered for centuries . . .

Here, 3,000 years later in the 1920's, is the ARCHAEOLOGIST from New York's Metropolitan Museum. After years of studying books and deciphering hieroglyphs and combing through hot sand in the desert, he uncovers the pit with the broken pieces of dozens of statues, including the SPHINX that was . . .

dumped there by the STEPSON,

marveled at by the EGYPTIAN PRIESTS,

chiseled by the SCULPTOR

and ordered by the PHARAOH.

Here is an agent from Egypt's

DEPARTMENT OF ANTIQUITIES,

which supervises the ancient site
and decides the Metropolitan Museum
will receive several statues,
including the partially put together
SPHINX that was . . .

found by the ARCHAEOLOGIST,

smashed and cracked by the STEPSON,

hailed by the EGYPTIAN PRIESTS,

made by the SCULPTOR

and ordered by the PHARAOH.

Here are the **ART MOVERS**, who meet the sphinx
when she comes to New York City by boat.
They oh-so-carefully load, cushion, and secure the statue
and thirteen boxes of pieces in their truck.

USA.

NEW YORK

Atlantic Ocean

EUROPE

EGYPT

Africa

Route SPHINX took

By avoiding bumpy roads and tight turns,
they safely deliver to the museum
the SPHINX that was . . .

released by the DEPARTMENT OF ANTIQUITIES,

identified by the ARCHAEOLOGIST,

busted up by the STEPSON,

honored by the EGYPTIAN PRIESTS,

created by the SCULPTOR

and ordered by the PHARAOH so long ago.

Here is the Metropolitan Museum's

CURATOR,

who knows a lot about ancient Egypt.
He can read and write hieroglyphs,
tell a fake when he sees one (usually),
and estimate how old a piece is
just by looking at it.
He plans where to place
and how to exhibit
the SPHINX that was . . .

delivered to New York by the **ART MOVERS**,

made available by the DEPARTMENT OF ANTIQUITIES,

unearthed by the ARCHAEOLOGIST,

destroyed by the STEPSON,

celebrated by the EGYPTIAN PRIESTS,

shaped by the SCULPTOR

and ordered by the PHARAOH.

Here are the museum's **conservators,**

who, with help from the curator, finish putting together the hundreds

of broken fragments, and fill in with plaster the many gaps and holes.

Back in one piece after 3,000 years

is the SPHINX of Hatshepsut that was . . .

the
mummy

plaster

GLUE

Box 1
sphinx

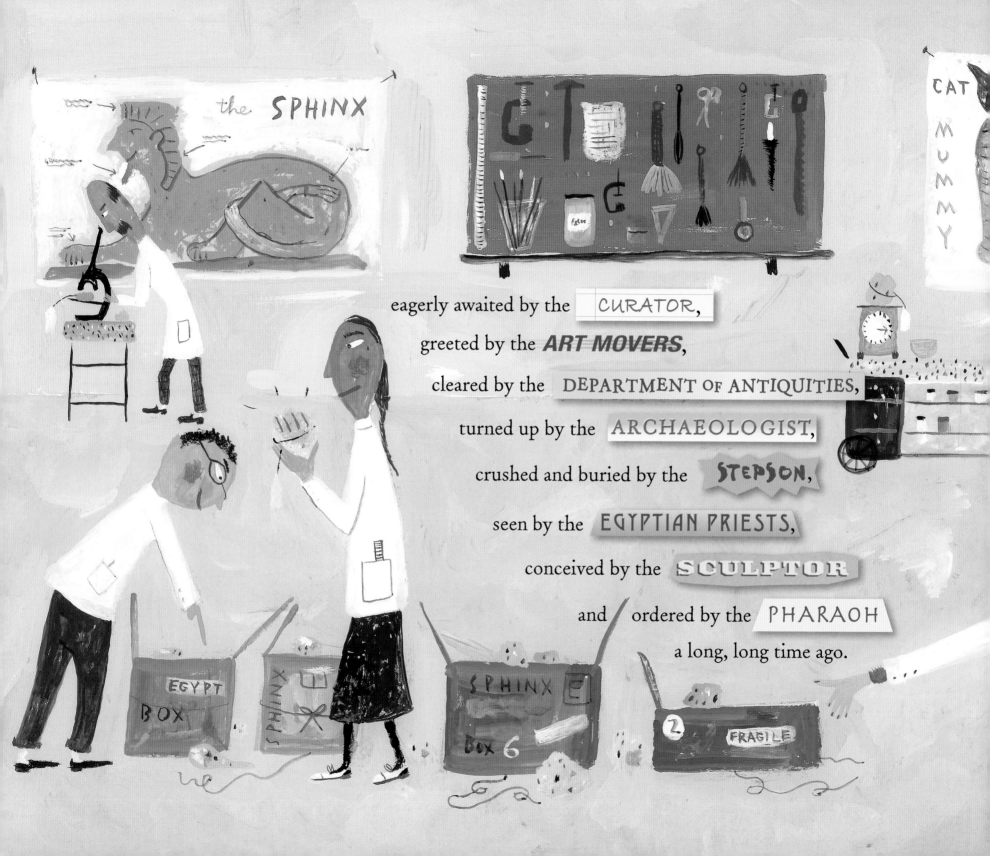

the SPHINX

CAT MUMMY

eagerly awaited by the CURATOR,

greeted by the *ART MOVERS*,

cleared by the DEPARTMENT OF ANTIQUITIES,

turned up by the ARCHAEOLOGIST,

crushed and buried by the STEPSON,

seen by the EGYPTIAN PRIESTS,

conceived by the SCULPTOR

and ordered by the PHARAOH

a long, long time ago.

EGYPT BOX

SPHINX

SPHINX BOX 6

2 FRAGILE

Here are the museum's

RIGGERS,

who operate the heavy equipment
needed to haul to the floor
the partially restored,
seven-ton SPHINX that was . . .

The American WING →

put back together by the *conservators,*

researched by the CURATOR,

secured by the ***ART MOVERS***,

supervised by the DEPARTMENT OF ANTIQUITIES,

found in a pit by the ARCHAEOLOGIST,

left to be forgotten by the STEPSON,

observed by the EGYPTIAN PRIESTS,

produced by the SCULPTOR

and ordered by the PHARAOH.

Here is the REGISTRAR,

who notates for the museum's records the newest acquisition:

its measurements, weight, date, and origin.

Using red oil paint and a teeny, tiny brush,

he paints the official number (31.3.166) on the SPHINX that was . . .

hauled by the **RIGGERS**,

assembled by the *conservators,*

studied by the CURATOR,

loaded with care by the ***ART MOVERS***,

sent on its way by the DEPARTMENT OF ANTIQUITIES,

dug up by the ARCHAEOLOGIST,

shattered to bits by the STEPSON,

respected by the EGYPTIAN PRIESTS,

fabricated by the SCULPTOR

and ordered by the PHARAOH.

To the EGYPTIAN collection

Here is the *Artist* who paints the plaster-filled parts to look like the granite. But not exactly! It's important to be able to see which parts are real and which have been painted to look real.

Almost ready for public viewing is the SPHINX that was . . .

minutely numbered by the REGISTRAR,

positioned just so by the **RIGGERS**,

mended by the *conservators*,

planned for exhibit by the CURATOR,

moved to the museum by the *ART MOVERS*,

overseen by the DEPARTMENT OF ANTIQUITIES,

brought to light by the ARCHAEOLOGIST,

demolished by the STEPSON,

gazed at by the EGYPTIAN PRIESTS,

executed by the SCULPTOR

and ordered by the PHARAOH.

WET PAINT

MUMMY

Here is the PHOTOGRAPHER, who takes
the official photographs for the museum's records.
She takes some shots from this angle, some from that,
some in black and white, and some in color
of the SPHINX that was ...

retouched by the *Artist*,

assigned a number by the REGISTRAR,

hoisted and lowered by the **RIGGERS**,

rebuilt by the *conservators*,

examined by the CURATOR,

transported to New York by the ***ART MOVERS***,

surveyed by Egypt's DEPARTMENT OF ANTIQUITIES,

discovered in the 1920's by the ARCHAEOLOGIST,

wrecked by the STEPSON,

looked at by the EGYPTIAN PRIESTS,

formed by the SCULPTOR

and ordered by the PHARAOH

in ancient Egypt.

galleries 7 - 15

Here is the **Docent**, who loves museums, has read all about ancient Egypt,

and likes to talk to visitors about the SPHINX that was . . .

documented by the **PHOTOGRAPHER,**

painted and restored by the *Artist,*

officially numbered by the REGISTRAR,

carefully lifted by the **RIGGERS,**

repaired by the *conservators,*

welcomed by the CURATOR,

packed and unpacked by the ***ART MOVERS,***

approved by the DEPARTMENT OF ANTIQUITIES,

uncovered by the ARCHAEOLOGIST,

broken by the STEPSON,

prized by the EGYPTIAN PRIESTS,

carved by the SCULPTOR

and ordered by the PHARAOH . . .

More History

No one alive today can ever be 100% sure of events that occurred thousands of years ago. Fortunately, archaeologists, historians, and—in the case of Hatshepsut—Egyptologists, have studied and worked for years and years to make the fascinating past come alive for us.

The part of this book when Hatshepsut orders several statues from the sculptor is somewhat made up. No one really knows exactly how this happened. However, we do know from reading ancient Egyptian inscriptions that sphinxes were created to guard temples, and that Hatshepsut's temple served not only as a place to honor her memory but also to worship several gods.

The magnificent statues of Hatshepsut only stood in the temple for about 20 years before they were smashed and buried. Why the stepson, Thutmose III, destroyed them will never be definitively known. But he wasn't successful in erasing Hatshepsut's legacy, as little by little Egyptologists were able to piece together her history.

• In the third century B.C., Manetho, an Egyptian priest, mentioned a female pharaoh in his history of Dynasty 18, Egypt.

• In the 1890's, French archaeologist Edouard Naville excavated Hatshepsut's temple, which was partly buried.

• In 1903, archaeologist Howard Carter (the man responsible for the discovery of King Tutankhamun's famous tomb) found one of Hatshepsut's sarcophagi in the Valley of the Kings.

• AND—as you've just read about in this book—during the 1920's, Herbert E. Winlock and his team from The Metropolitan Museum of Art discovered the pit where they found the destroyed pieces of Hatshepsut's statues, including six colossal granite sphinxes!

The search for knowledge about ancient Egypt continues. In 2007, Hatshepsut's mummy was identified—using a missing tooth—by a team led by Egyptian archaeologist Zahi Hawass. Just think of what else can be uncovered in time!

Additional Facts and Figures

In the world of museum jobs, there was, and is, overlap within many different departments and job titles. For example, Herbert E. Winlock, the archaeologist who found the pit in Egypt at Deir el-Bahri with the remains of the Hatshepsut statues, was an Egyptologist and worked as a curator in The Metropolitan Museum of Art. He later became director of the entire Met!

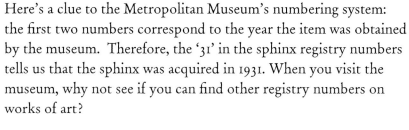

In 1922-29, the excavators from New York's Metropolitan Museum discovered and uncovered the remains of Hatshepsut's statuary. The fragments were patiently and painstakingly reassembled by the museum's crew in Egypt, and by 1931 their work was complete. Egypt's Department of Antiquities then divided the statues between the Egyptian Museum in Cairo and The Metropolitan Museum in New York.

Egypt's Department of Antiquities is now called The Supreme Council of Antiquities, and today all finds made in Egypt stay in the country.

The artist in the story was actually another member of the conservation staff.

SPHINX STATS:
  Length: 11 feet, 3 inches
  Height: 5 feet, 4.5 inches
  Weight: more than 7 tons!

Here's a clue to the Metropolitan Museum's numbering system: the first two numbers correspond to the year the item was obtained by the museum. Therefore, the '31' in the sphinx registry numbers tells us that the sphinx was acquired in 1931. When you visit the museum, why not see if you can find other registry numbers on works of art?

Today

You might be wondering where the other granite sphinxes from this set are today. One is at the Ägyptisches Museum in Berlin, Germany; two (plus broken pieces from another) are at the Egyptian Museum in Cairo. The Met also has one that is incomplete. Additionally, Hatshepsut had other sets of sphinxes not even mentioned in this story.

Hatshepsut's restored temple in Thebes, now called Luxor, is open to the public and is one of the most famous sites in Egypt.

If you ever travel to New York City, visit the Metropolitan Museum and see the sphinx of Hatshepsut, for now you know the story of "How the Sphinx Got to the Museum."